WHICH CAME FIRST?

TRANSPORTATION INVENTIONS

FROM SUBWAYS TO SUBMARINES

by Sandra Will

Consultant: Paul F. Johnston, Washington, D.C.

BEARPORT
PUBLISHING COMPANY, INC.

New York, New York

Credits
Cover and title page, Michelle Barbera (illustrator), Red Barn Studio/istockphoto (train), José Carlos
Pires Pereira/istockphoto (bus); 4, Steve Thornton/Corbis; 5(t), Andre Jenny/Alamy; 5(b), Tibor
Bognar/Alamy; 6, Steven Poe/Alamy; 7(t), Kevin Fleming/Corbis; 7(b), Fine Art Photographic
Library/Corbis; 8, Hugh Beebower/Corbis; 9(t), Atmosphere Picture Library/Alamy; 9(b), Kevin
Foy/Alamy; 10, John Violet/Alamy; 11(t), Jon Bower/Alamy; 11(b), Mike Brinson/The Image Bank/
Getty Images; 12, CORBIS; 13(t), James Cheadle/Alamy; 13(b), Photo Japan/Alamy; 14, Bettmann/
Corbis; 15(t), Stock Connection Distribution/Alamy; 15(b), Transtock Inc./Alamy; 16, National
Archive/Newsmakers/Getty Images; 17(t), Georgina Bowater/Corbis; 17(b), Ambient Images
Inc./Alamy; 18, f1 online/Alamy; 19(t), S Burbridge/Alamy; 19(b), Powered by Light/Alan Spencer/
Alamy; 20, CORBIS; 21(t), Giles Robberts/Alamy; 21(b), Chris Bland; Eye Ubiquitous/Corbis;
22, Bettmann/Corbis; 23(t), NASA; 23(b), Jonathan Chandler/US Navy/Reuters/Corbis; 24, David
Dyson/Getty Images; 25(t), Kevin Foy/Alamy; 25(b), ANDREW WONG/Reuters/Corbis.

Design and production by Dawn Beard Creative and Octavo Design and Production, Inc.

Library of Congress Cataloging-in-Publication Data

Will, Sandra.
  Transportation inventions : from subways to submarines / by Sandra Will.
     p. cm. — (Which came first?)
  Includes bibliographical references and index.
  ISBN 1-59716-133-0 (library binding) — ISBN 1-59716-140-3 (pbk.)
  1. Motor vehicles—Juvenile literature. 2. Transportation—Juvenile literature.
I. Title. II. Series.

TL147.W5335 2006
629.04—dc22
                            2005030941

For more information, write to Bearport Publishing Company, Inc., 101 Fifth Avenue, Suite 6R,
New York, New York 10003. Printed in the United States of America.

1 2 3 4 5 6 7 8 9 10

Contents

9

5

17

19

23

Introduction

Hundreds of years ago, it took months to travel to faraway places. Why? The car and plane hadn't been invented yet. People mainly traveled using horses or boats—or just by walking. These were slow ways of getting from place to place.

Since then, people have looked for new ways to travel that are faster and more **efficient**. Today, a person can fly around the world in less than two days.

This book describes ten pairs of **transportation** inventions. Read about each pair and guess which one came first. Then turn the page for the answer.

▲ **Before trains were invented, many people used stagecoaches to take long journeys.**

Turn the page to
find out which
came first.

Which Came First?

Canoe

The first canoes were made of wood. People used them to travel long distances. Today, canoes are made of wood, aluminum, or other materials. These small lightweight boats are a fun way to watch wildlife along a river.

▲ **People use paddles to move and steer canoes.**

Rickshaw

Imagine moving through a crowded street in a cart pulled by another person. You'd be traveling in a rickshaw. Rickshaws were once widely used in **Asia**.

◄ **Many tourists take rickshaw rides to experience the sights of the city they are visiting.**

Answer: Canoe

Native people of North America built and **developed** the canoe over thousands of years. In the 1700s, the boats became a popular way for North American traders to transport **goods**. Canoes were an easy way to travel through lakes and rivers.

Rickshaws were first widely used around 1868 in Japan. By the 1870s, they had become the main form of public transportation in Japanese cities.

Early canoes were made from tree trunks. People dug out the insides of the trunks so that they could sit in them. The word "canoe" comes from the word "kenu," which means "dugout."

Which Came First?

Turn the page to find out which came first.

Steamboat

Before railroads became popular, steamboats were the best way to transport goods and people. They carried cotton, sugar, and other **agricultural** supplies on major American rivers—like the Mississippi.

Stagecoach

Stagecoaches were used to carry the mail as well as people. As a result, they were also known as "mail coaches." Like steamboats, stagecoaches were eventually replaced by the railroad.

▲ **This stagecoach was used to deliver mail in England.**

7

Answer: Subway

Andrew Smith Hallidie built the first successful cable car in San Francisco in 1873. Yet the first passenger subway system opened ten years earlier, in 1863. It was the Metropolitan Railway in London. The first American subway opened in Boston in 1897.

▲ **London's Underground is the world's oldest subway system.**

More people ride the Moscow subway system than any other in the world. About 3.2 billion people travel on it each year.

Turn the page to
find out which
came first.

Which Came First?

Bicycle

There are more than one billion bicycles in the world today. People usually ride them just for fun. Yet in China and other countries, many people ride bikes to get to work every day.

▲ **Bicycle riders in China**

▲ **The "deck" is the part of the skateboard that riders stand on.**

Skateboard

California surfers used wooden boards and roller skates to create the first skateboards. Riding them made surfers feel like they were riding a wave.

11

Answer: Bicycle

The bicycle was first introduced in Germany around 1816. Very early bikes were made of wood and had no pedals. Riders had to push against the ground to make the machines go. Pedals were added in 1839. Skateboards did not come onto the scene until the 1950s.

◀ **Bicycle without pedals in 1827**

In the 1850s and 1860s, bicycles had wooden wheels with tires made of iron. Rubber tires filled with air were not common until around 1895.

Turn the page to
find out which
came first.

Which Came First?

Motorcycle

Motorcycles are like bicycles. They both have two wheels and handlebars. However, motorcycles have engines and can travel as fast as cars.

Car

Today, most car engines are powered by gasoline. At one time, however, there were steam-powered cars. Unfortunately, they often blew up.

▲ **These experimental electric mini-cars are recharging their batteries.**

Answer: Motorcycle

It's almost a tie! In 1885, German engineer Gottleib Daimler invented a vehicle with two main wheels that ran on gas—a motorcycle. The first motorcycle to be made in large quantities, however, was created in 1894.

By 1886, Karl Benz got a **patent** for a three-wheeled vehicle powered by gas—a car. Daimler invented a car that same year, but his had four wheels.

A steam-powered car was first invented in France in 1769. It traveled about two and a half miles per hour (4 kph). The first practical and successful cars, however, were powered by gas.

▲ **This is what the first gas-powered motorcycle looked like.**

Which Came First?

Turn the page to find out which came first.

Airplane

Airplanes are the fastest way to transport people, mail, or goods. Today, many jumbo jets can carry 600 passengers. The first planes, however, could carry only one person at a time.

▲ **The Boeing 747 is commonly known as a jumbo jet. It is a large passenger airplane that travels at about 565 miles per hour (909 kph).**

▲ **Nicknames for helicopters include "chopper," "eggbeater," and "whirlybird."**

Helicopter

Unlike planes, helicopters can fly forward or backward, straight up or down, and even sideways. They can also **hover**, which makes them great for rescue missions.

15

Answer: Airplane

In 1903, Orville and Wilbur Wright developed the first practical engine-powered airplane. It went 30 miles per hour (48 kph). The first flight lasted about 12 seconds. By 1905, they had built a plane that could fly for more than half an hour.

The first helicopter flown by a pilot was invented in 1907. Yet it took until about 1939 for the modern helicopter to be developed.

▲ **The Wright brothers' 1903 plane during its first flight at Kitty Hawk, North Carolina**

The first jumbo-jet flight that carried paying passengers took place in 1970. It flew from New York to London.

Which Came First?

Turn the page to find out which came first.

Train

Today, trains use electricity and diesel fuel to run. The earliest ones, however, were pulled by steam engines.

◀ **The TGV is one of the fastest electric trains. It travels at an average speed of 186 miles per hour (299 kph).**

Bus

Carriages pulled by horses were an early kind of city bus. In fact, they were called "omnibuses," which means "for all." Like today's buses, they ran along specific **routes**. In time, however, these horse-drawn carriages were replaced by buses with gas engines.

Answer: Train

The first steam **locomotive** was built in England by Richard Trevithick in 1804. It was called the "puffing devil." Early steam engines were used to pull coal wagons in Britain. Yet by 1830, people in America and England could begin traveling on trains.

Buses powered by gas weren't invented until the 1890s in Germany. They were cars that had been made longer to hold extra passengers.

▲ **Steam trains became more popular than stagecoaches and steamboats because they carried goods and people longer distances in a shorter period of time.**

The first regular motorized-bus service in the United States began in New York City in 1905.

Which Came First?

Turn the page to find out which came first.

Submarine

A submarine is a kind of boat that can travel on the **surface** of water or down below. Most submarines are used by the military. However, scientists also use them to do underwater research.

Hovercraft

How do people travel over land and water in the same vehicle? They ride in a hovercraft. A hovercraft blows jets of air downward. This force pushes the vehicle upward so that it can move above land or water.

Answer: Submarine

British inventor Christopher Cockerell made the first useful hovercraft in 1956. As far back as the 1600s, however, there were many early attempts to create a submarine. Most did not succeed. The first military submarine was used during the American Revolution (1775–1783). It was called the *Turtle*, and it was powered with a hand crank. Only one person could fit in it. Submarines did not become effective weapons until the 1900s.

▲ **U.S. submarine patrolling the Pacific Ocean in 1945**

A Dutch doctor, Cornelius van Drebbel, built an early type of submarine in the 1620s. He took a wooden rowboat and covered it in leather. Air tubes were used for breathing.

Which Came First?

Turn the page to find out which came first.

Escalator

An escalator is a moving staircase that takes people up or down. Escalators are most often used in department stores or shopping malls.

◀ **The original escalators were made of wood. Today, escalators are made of metal.**

Elevator

Elevators didn't just change the way people moved. They changed the way cities were built. Without elevators, most buildings wouldn't be very tall.

21

Answer: Elevator

The earliest working escalator was introduced as a ride in Coney Island around 1895. By 1900, escalators were being used in department stores and train stations.

Early steam-powered elevators, however, were already in use by the 1840s. They carried **freight**, however, not people. The first elevator for passenger use was installed in a New York City department store in 1857.

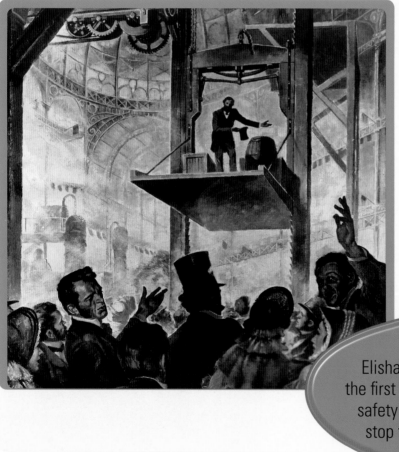

◄ Elisha Graves Otis shows off his first elevator in New York.

In the early 1850s, Elisha Graves Otis invented the first elevator that had a safety device. The device would stop the elevator from falling if its cable broke.

Turn the page to
find out which
came first.

Which Came First?

Space Shuttle

Space shuttles take off like rockets but glide back to Earth like airplanes. So they can be used more than once. Astronauts aboard shuttles repair satellites and conduct space experiments.

▲ A cloud sometimes forms around a plane when it goes faster than the speed of sound.

Supersonic Plane

Supersonic planes can go faster than the speed of sound— 761 miles per hour (1,225 kph). Early supersonic planes were designed for the military by American and British engineers.

Answer: Supersonic Plane

NASA (National Aeronautics and Space Administration) launched the first space shuttle mission in 1981. Chuck Yeager flew a plane faster than the speed of sound, however, in 1947.

At first, supersonic planes were used only by the military. Yet in 1976, one of the first supersonic passenger planes began service. It was called the Concorde. In 2000, a Concorde crashed as it was taking off. The planes stopped flying three years later.

▲ **The Concorde**

Chuck Yeager's plane, *Glamorous Glennis*, was named after his wife.

Which Comes Next?

Here are two new transportation ideas that inventors have come up with. Which one do you think will become a popular way to travel?

Maglev Train

Imagine a train that runs without an engine or wheels. Meet the maglev, a train that uses powerful **magnets** to float above the track and to travel at super-fast speeds.

◀ **The world's first maglev train carried passengers from Shanghai's Pudong Airport to downtown Shanghai at a speed of up to 267 miles per hour (430 kph).**

Hy-wire Car

Here's a car that doesn't use gasoline to run. How does it work? Its motor is powered by changing **hydrogen** and oxygen into electricity. So it doesn't create air pollution.

Scorecard

How many did you get correct?

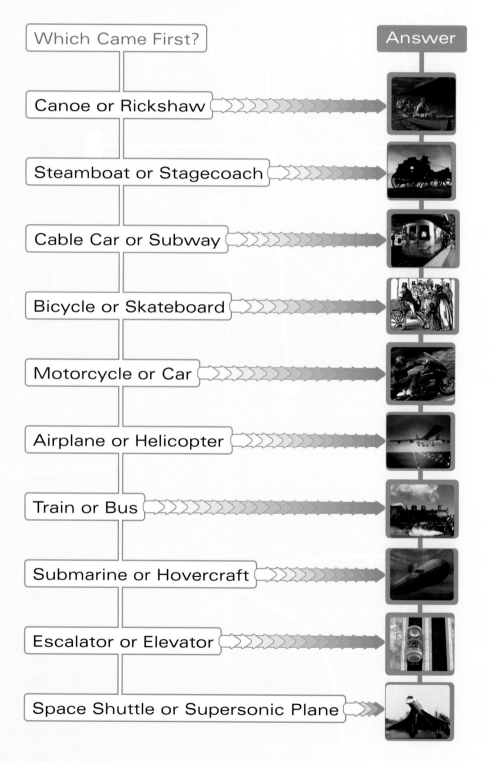

Which Came First?	Answer
Canoe or Rickshaw	
Steamboat or Stagecoach	
Cable Car or Subway	
Bicycle or Skateboard	
Motorcycle or Car	
Airplane or Helicopter	
Train or Bus	
Submarine or Hovercraft	
Escalator or Elevator	
Space Shuttle or Supersonic Plane	

Bonus Questions

Now you know which of the transportation inventions in this book came first. Here are a few bonus questions.

1. **The wheel is an important part of most types of transportation. How old is the wheel?**

   a. more than 5,000 years old c. 1,000 years old

   b. 2,000 years old d. 600 years old

2. **Most cars run on gasoline, but some newer cars run on gasoline and batteries. What are they called?**

   a. electric cars c. hybrid cars

   b. gasobattery cars d. combination cars

3. **Which airport is visited by the most people?**

   a. London, England c. Paris, France

   b. New York, New York d. Atlanta, Georgia

4. **The longest train in the world is 1.8 miles long (2.9 km) and runs in**

   a. the United States c. Russia

   b. Africa d. Japan

Just the Facts

❋ In 1997, the Thrust SSC became the first supersonic car when it reached a top speed of 766 miles per hour (1,233 kph).

❋ The latest development in helicopters is called the tiltrotor. It can fly as fast as some planes. However, it takes off and lands straight up and down like a helicopter.

❋ In 1912, Lester Wire, a policeman in Salt Lake City, Utah, invented one of the first electric traffic lights. It had only red and green lights. In 1920, yellow lights were added.

❋ The longest escalator in the world is in Hong Kong, China. It has four sections and is 745 feet (227 m) long.

❋ The Gibbs Aquada is a car—and a boat! It can drive on land, but with a flick of a switch, it turns into a boat to carry people across water. It doesn't have doors, so water can't leak in.

The History of Transportation Inventions

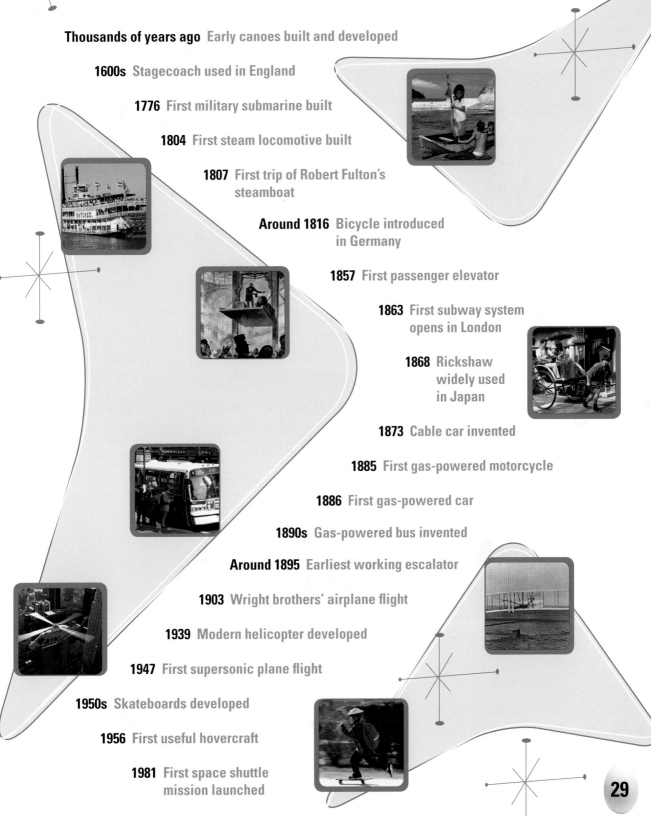

Thousands of years ago Early canoes built and developed

1600s Stagecoach used in England

1776 First military submarine built

1804 First steam locomotive built

1807 First trip of Robert Fulton's steamboat

Around 1816 Bicycle introduced in Germany

1857 First passenger elevator

1863 First subway system opens in London

1868 Rickshaw widely used in Japan

1873 Cable car invented

1885 First gas-powered motorcycle

1886 First gas-powered car

1890s Gas-powered bus invented

Around 1895 Earliest working escalator

1903 Wright brothers' airplane flight

1939 Modern helicopter developed

1947 First supersonic plane flight

1950s Skateboards developed

1956 First useful hovercraft

1981 First space shuttle mission launched

Glossary

agricultural (*ag*-ruh-KUL-chur-uhl)   having to do with farming or farms

Asia (AY-zhuh)   the largest continent on Earth; it is made up of 50 countries, including China, India, and part of Russia

cables (KAY-buhlz)   thick ropes or wires

carriages (KA-rij-iz)   vehicles that have wheels, often pulled by horses

developed (di-VEL-uhpt)   made changes to something to make it more advanced

efficient (uh-FISH-uhnt)   able to get a job done well without wasting time or energy

engineer (en-juh-NIHR)   a person who designs and builds things, such as machines, bridges, vehicles, and roads

financially (fye-NANCH-uh-lee)   having to do with money

freight (FRAYT)   cargo or supplies

goods (GUDZ)   things that are sold

hover (HUHV-ur)   to stay in the air in one place

hydrogen (HYE-druh-juhn)   a gas

locomotive (*loh*-kuh-MOH-tiv)   an engine used to push or pull railroad cars

magnets (MAG-nits)   pieces of metal that attract other metals

native (NAY-tiv)   a person born in a particular place

patent (PAT-uhnt)   an official document giving inventors special rights to their inventions

routes (ROOTS)   roads or paths that one follows to get from place to place

supersonic (soo-pur-SON-ik)   a speed that is faster than the speed of sound

surface (SUR-fiss)   the top or outside of something

transportation (*transs*-pur-TAY-shuhn)   a way or system of moving people and goods from place to place

vehicles (VEE-uh-kuhlz)   things that carry people or goods from place to place

Bibliography

Lopez, Donald, ed. *Flight.* San Francisco, CA: Barnes and Noble (2003).

Wood, Richard, ed. *Great Inventions.* San Francisco, CA: Barnes and Noble (2003).

www.bts.gov

www.hybridcars.com/technology.html

www.mta.nyc.ny.us

www.nationmaster.com/encyclopedia/Stagecoach

www.waterspirits.com/history.html

Read More

Brimner, Larry Dane. *Subway: The Story of Tunnels, Tubes, and Tracks.* Honesdale, PA: Boyds Mills Press (2004).

Carson, Mary Kay. *The Wright Brothers for Kids: How They Invented the Airplane.* Chicago, IL: Chicago Review Press (2003).

Coiley, John. *Eyewitness: Train.* New York: DK Publishing (2000).

Sutton, Richard. *Eyewitness: Car.* New York: DK Publishing (2005).

Wilson, Anthony. *Visual Timeline of Transportation.* New York: DK Publishing (1995).

Learn More Online

Visit these Web sites to learn more about transportation inventions:

http://inventors.about.com/library/inventors/bl_history_of_transportation.htm

www.si.edu/resource/faq/nmah/transportation.htm

Index

About the Author

When Sandra Will is not writing children's books, she enjoys reading books, visiting museums, watching good sporting events, and playing with her dog, Maggie. Originally from Chehalis, Washington, Sandra lives in New York City.